Lasse Skaksen

Reverse logistics. An analysis

GRIN Verlag

Bibliografische Information der Deutschen Nationalbibliothek:

Die Deutsche Bibliothek verzeichnet diese Publikation in der Deutschen National-
bibliografie; detaillierte bibliografische Daten sind im Internet über http://dnb.d-
nb.de/ abrufbar.

Dieses Werk sowie alle darin enthaltenen einzelnen Beiträge und Abbildungen
sind urheberrechtlich geschützt. Jede Verwertung, die nicht ausdrücklich vom
Urheberrechtsschutz zugelassen ist, bedarf der vorherigen Zustimmung des Verla-
ges. Das gilt insbesondere für Vervielfältigungen, Bearbeitungen, Übersetzungen,
Mikroverfilmungen, Auswertungen durch Datenbanken und für die Einspeicherung
und Verarbeitung in elektronische Systeme. Alle Rechte, auch die des auszugsweisen
Nachdrucks, der fotomechanischen Wiedergabe (einschließlich Mikrokopie) sowie
der Auswertung durch Datenbanken oder ähnliche Einrichtungen, vorbehalten.

Imprint:

Copyright © 2011 GRIN Verlag GmbH
Druck und Bindung: Books on Demand GmbH, Norderstedt Germany
ISBN: 978-3-656-49532-1

This book at GRIN:

http://www.grin.com/en/e-book/232612/reverse-logistics-an-analysis

GRIN - Your knowledge has value

Der GRIN Verlag publiziert seit 1998 wissenschaftliche Arbeiten von Studenten, Hochschullehrern und anderen Akademikern als eBook und gedrucktes Buch. Die Verlagswebsite www.grin.com ist die ideale Plattform zur Veröffentlichung von Hausarbeiten, Abschlussarbeiten, wissenschaftlichen Aufsätzen, Dissertationen und Fachbüchern.

Visit us on the internet:

http://www.grin.com/

http://www.facebook.com/grincom

http://www.twitter.com/grin_com

Individual Research Report

From: **Mr. Lasse T. Skaksen**

Course: **Global Business Logistics**

Subject: **Individual Research Report – Reverse Logistics**

Date: **14/11/2011**

Table of Contents

1.0 Introduction

In the medium term challenges for global business logistics managers are many. These are driven by external factors as well as internal motives.

This research report will describe, analyse and evaluate an increasingly relevant topic within global business logics, namely *Reverse Logistics*. Two main external drivers as well as the major internal motives to establish a Reverse Logistics network will be identified and examined.

The following definition of Reverse Logistics by Hawks will be utilized in this report: "the process of planning, implementing, and controlling the efficient, cost effective flow of raw materials, in-process inventory, finished goods and related information from the point of consumption to the point of origin for the purpose of recapturing value or proper disposal" (Hawks, 2006).

Furthermore the relevance of Reverse Logistics is underlined when considering the research by Tierney (Tierney S., 2004) and the findings by DuPont (Weel, 2010) jointly; Tierney established that the costs related to Reverse Logistics was up to four times higher than delivering the product to the costumer in the first place. This is in particular interesting when the DuPont analysis established that a 2% savings in cost can generate an up to 25% increase in RONA[1]. In addition it has been shown that the cost of repairs can be reduced by 10% with the implementation of an efficient Reverse Logistics network (Tatham 2011)

A comparison of traditional logistics, i.e. "forward logistics" and reverse logistics will be given to build an understanding of the new and different challenges reverse logistics impose on managers. Lastly the research report will identify, analyse and evaluate the new managerial decisions global logistics managers will face in a future with Reverse Logistics as a well established and significant part of the supply network.

Underneath is a graphic depiction of the Reverse Logistics network.

---

[1]Return On Net Assets

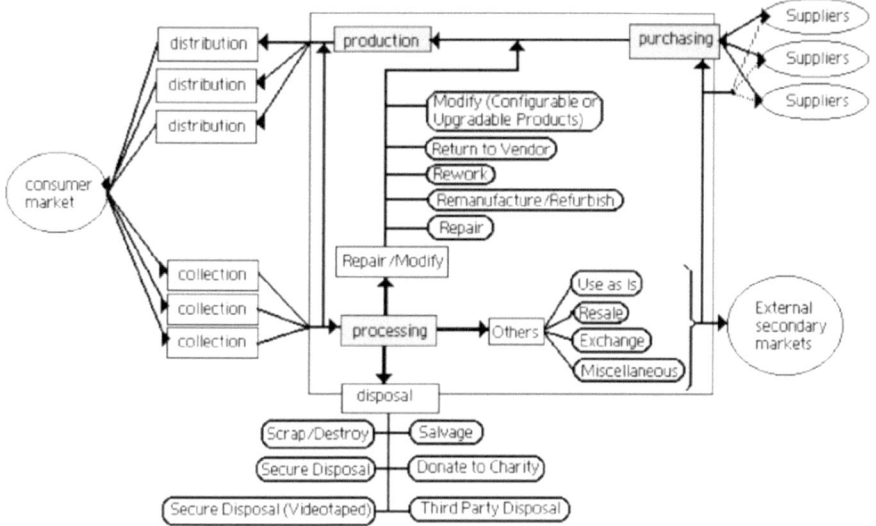

Source: Soto Zuluaga, 2006.

2.0 External drivers of Reverse Logistics

Underneath are discussed two external drivers of the implementation of Reverse Logistics, namely legislation and environmental concerns/CSR. The factors have been identified as the main external drivers of the recent increased focus on Reverse Logistics. (Kokkinaki et al., 2002). A number of other drivers and motivators are borderline external/internal, the most important of these will be discussed under the internal factors.

2.1 Legislation

Climate change is the significant and lasting change in local or global weather conditions brought about by natural and manmade factors (Cuevas, 2011 pp 29-30). During the last years it is increasingly accepted that a large part of the climate change is in fact manmade. Legislators are therefore attempting to regulate and control undesired non sustainable behaviour by firms. New taxes such as the "Australian carbon tax" and the European WEEE (http://ec.europa.eu) directive are examples of such attempts. The WEEE directive is aimed at reducing waste, keeping hazardous material out of landfills and promote the reuse of scarce resources such as ferrous metals, aluminium and copper (Deffree S., 2008). In relation to Reverse Logistics the WEEE directive is highly relevant, as the WEEE directive in practise imposes on Electrical and

Electronic Equipment (EEE) manufacturers to create a Reverse Logistics network (Rivlin K. et al, 2005). Legislation will continue to be a driver in the future. Legislation such as or similar to the WEEE directive is already being considered in other countries and regions. Latest, Ontario joined other Canadian provinces such as Alberta, Nova Scotia and Saskatchewan when introducing a WEEE directive (Deffree S., 2008).

2.2 CSR - Stakeholder expectations and requirements

Stakeholders, from consumer to shareholder, are increasingly expecting firms to behave in a socially responsible way. This includes expectations and requirements to how a firm manages the impact it has on the environment. Not only when producing and delivering the product or service, but in its entire lifecycle including disposal. (Tibben-Lembke, R.S., 2002, Moellenkopf et al., 2010, Skinner et al. 2008 and Smith, 2005) Also, shareholders are very aware that recent studies reveal that firms with well functioning CSR practices financially outperform other firms (Burke & Logsdon, 1996, Peters & Mullen, 2009, Shen & Chang, 2009 and Gupta & Sharma, 2009). Concurrently consumers are increasingly conscious about the environmental impact, hence pressure firms to take responsibility.

Reverse Logistics is an excellent way of signalling corporate social responsibility to consumers. Because consumers interact with the firm or its representatives, they get a "first row- hands on experience" with the CSR activities of firm. With relation to shareholders, it is obvious that this CSR practices not only meets customer expectations, but also the expectations of shareholders. Shareholders will without doubt think positively about initiatives that improve reputation and financial performance as well as improve resilience.

3.0 Internal motives to establish a Reverse Logistics network

In addition to the external drivers of Reverse Logistics there are several internal motives for global business logistics managers. These, one way or another, all evolve around either creating capabilities and sustainable competitive advantages or diminishing competitor advantages.

Rogers and Tibben-Lembke (Tibben-Lembke, R. S & Rogers D.S., 1998) have identified four internal motives for firms to create a Reverse Logistics flow. The table underneath depicts how large a percentage of the respondents replied that the mentioned factor is a driver/motive for their Reverse Logistics network.

Driver/Motivation	Percentage
Competition	65 %
Clearing channels	33 %
Value recapturing	28 %
Asset recovery	26 %

Table 1 Roger and Tibben-Lembke, 1998

- Competition; Meeting and or exceeding customer expectations better or more efficiently than competitors is a competitive advantage. By creating an efficient Reverse Logistics network a firm can differentiate itself from competitors and create a strong relationship with costumers. (Smith, 2005, Skinner et al. 2008) As consumers expectations to the CSR conduct of the company increases, so will the importance of Reverse Logistics as a competitive parameter. Both Moellenkopf and Dutton (Dutton G., 2010 and Moellenkopf et al. 2010) supports the argument that firms can create competitive advantages by differentiating themselves as an ethical and CSR sound firm. Other competitive advantages could be securing supply and reducing costs. Finally it has been established that companies who engage in CSR, which Reverse Logistics to a certain degree is, improves financial performance (Burke & Logsdon, 1996, Peters & Mullen, 2009, Shen & Chang, 2009 and Gupta & Sharma, 2009)

  Furthermore, by implementing a successful Reverse Logistics network the cost of repairs can be reduced by up to 10% and cycle times from 17 to 4 days. This will lead to higher profit margins and higher customer satisfaction. (Tatham (2011)

- Clearing channels; 33% of respondents reported that a motive for their Reverse Logistics network is to clear channels. I.e. effectively enabling retailers or distributors to return obsolete products, which again allows the producing firm to more easily push new products forward through the supply chain network – as customers will seek to fill the shelves again.

- Value recapturing and Asset recovery; depending on industry and the lifecycle of the product, value recapturing can also be a means to a competitive advantage. In addition to being a legal requirement in the EEE industry, a successful Reverse Logistics network can also assist the firm in securing supply of scarce resources and depending on the efficiency of the network reduce costs related to acquiring the resources. (Halldorson A., 2008)

  Research has furthermore found that up to 39% of products returned can be sold as is, re-packed and sold as is, sold to broker or sold to outlet store (Tatham (2011).

- Legislation; even though this is mentioned as an external driver above, it can be argued that some firms "internalize the driver". Firms acknowledge that legislation will continuously become stricter and for two reasons they will attempt to stay one step ahead, i.e. do more than what they are legally obligated to do. The first reason being that the firm to a higher degree can set the pace of the changes and are not forced into transformational changes. The second reason is to use the "halo position" to brand itself to customers which we established above will lead to competitive advantages.

4.0 Forward logistics vs. Reverse Logistics

To support point *5.0 management Challenges* in this research report, this section will elaborate on the main differences between classic forward logistics and Reverse Logistics. Understanding the differences between the two components of a modern supply network, will lead to a better and deeper understanding of the challenges global logistics managers will face in the future, where Reverse Logistics with no doubt will have a more prominent role in supply network management.

4.1 Differences

The following table sums up the differences between forward and Reverse Logistics.

Forward	Reverse
Forecasting relatively straightforward	Forecasting more difficult
One to many transportation	Many to one transportation
Product quality uniform	Product quality not uniform
Product packaging uniform	Product packaging often damaged
Destination/routing clear	Destination/routing unclear
Standardized channel	Exception driven
Disposition options clear	Disposition not clear
Pricing relatively uniform	Pricing dependent on many factors
Importance of speed recognized	Speed often not considered a priority
Forward distribution costs closely monitored by accounting systems	Reverse costs less directly visible
Inventory management consistent	Inventory management not consistent
Product lifecycle manageable	Product lifecycle issues more complex
Negotiation between parties straightforward	Negotiation complicated by additional considerations
Marketing methods well-known	Marketing complicated by several factors
Real-time information readily available to track product	Visibility of process less transparent

Figure 1 (Rogers, D. S., Tibben-Lembke, R. S. 2002)

The most significant difference between forward logistics and Reverse Logistics is the fact that forward logistics networks are demand dependant whereas Reverse Logistics networks are supply dependant. A forward logistic network is dependent on customer demand to pull products forward in the chain. A Reverse Logistics network is dependent on customer's to push products back through the supply chain. This should not be interpreted as an argument that all forward logistics chains are based on a "pull" system. Products may well be "pushed" through a forward logistics network, but are in the end dependent on customer demand. Neither should it be interpreted in the way that forward logistics networks are not dependent on supply – but a forward logistics network are better able to manage supplies. (Lourenço and Soto, 2002 and Kokkinaki et al., 2002) "Supply" or return from customers are more volatile and unpredictable than supplies from other firms.

Another major difference between the two flows is the degree of uncertainty and predictability. In a forward logistics network factors such as demand, product quality and optimal routing are reasonably forecast able, hence appropriate measures can be taken to minimize cost and concurrently deliver a consistent product to customers. In the Reverse Logistics network the previous mentioned factors are harder to forecast, hence harder to plan accordingly and thereby difficult to optimize processes and customer experience.

Lastly, another significant difference between forward and Reverse Logistics is the number of decision points, which is much higher in a Reverse Logistics network. This will, ceteris paribus, make the network more challenging to manage.(Tatham 2011)

4.2 Cost differences

Cost associated to	Reverse Logistics vs. Forward logistics costs
Transportation	Greater
Inventory holding cost	Lower
Shrinkage (theft)	Much lower
Obsolence	May be higher
Collection	Much higher – less standardized
Sorting, quality diagnosis	Much greater
Handling	Much higher
Refurbishment/repackaging	Significant for RL, non-existent for forward
Change from book value	Significant for RL, non-existent for forward

Figure 2 (Rogers, D. S., Tibben-Lembke, R. S. 2002)

Most of the differences in costs are self-explanatory, however a few comments should be made. *Transportation, collection and handling* are all higher due to unpredictability in both location, amount and quality of "supplies". Sorting, quality diagnosis and refurbishment/repackaging are higher due to variance in quality and condition. Both shrinkage and inventory holding costs are lower as the value of the product are lower. Obsolescence may be higher as there is a risk that the product can't be reused or refurbished, and will have to go to landfill. The unpredictability and uncertainty, leads to more decision points –which complicates and slows the process down.

Lastly, a difference between forward and Reverse Logistics is the inability to precisely connect costs with the different activities, i.e. locate cost drivers. This inability is clearly linked to 5.0 *Management Challenges*, as this if often caused by managers who does not pay sufficient attention to Reverse Logistic processes. Kwan Tan and Kumar (Kwan T. & Kumar, 2006) have therefore suggested a framework wherein Reverse Logistics costs are divided in 3 major groups.

(1) Unit costs include:
- Transport cost – cost incurred in local transport for each product return from customer to the manufacturer.
- Customs duty – cost incurred in clearing each product return at the customs.
- Acquisition cost – cost incurred to acquire each product return.
- Handling cost – cost incurred to track and document each product return.

(2) Variable costs depending on the quality of returns:
- Repair cost – cost incurred to repair each product return before it is sold.
- Reuse costs – cost incurred to repackage each product return before it is sold.
- Scrap cost – cost incurred to scrap each product return.

(3) Variable costs depending on the time of storage:
- Storage cost – cost incurred to store each product return.
- Freight cost – cost incurred to ship the product returns via air or sea.

The purpose of the framework is to enable managers to get an overview of the various cost drivers and where cost actually are incurred. The first step in managing is measuring. If you cannot measure precisely, you cannot manage efficiently.

5.0 Management challenges

Guide identified seven overall challenges connected to implementing a Reverse Logistic network. These are as follows: (Guide et al, 2002)

- Unpredictable timing and quantity of returns
- Balancing demands with returns
- Disassembling the returned products
- The uncertainty in materials recovered from returned items

- Requirement for a reverse logistics network
- Product matching restrictions
- The uncertainty of necessary routings materials undergoing repairs/remanufacturing operations and highly variable processing times.

These challenges are all somewhat different from the ones a global business logistics manager face when managing the forward logistics network. The first challenge is self-explanatory and was discussed in 3.0.

Balancing demands with returns refers to the challenge of balancing the actual returned products with the products the firm actually need. Because supplies cannot be controlled as in a forward logistics network, it is a challenge for the company to acquire the right amounts of the various products. Inventory management and production planning are more difficult when supplies cannot be controlled. *Disassembling the returned products* adds complexity to production planning and control as the degree of disassembly level depending on product is hard to predict.

The uncertainty in materials recovered from returned items is a challenge as the varying product quality leads to two identical products yielding different re-usable parts.

Requirement for a reverse logistics network is a very complex and often the hardest challenge to accommodate. This relates to the design requirements for the Reverse Logistics network, in regards to location and number of "return-centers", customer incentives, transportation modes and use of third party providers for one or more of the processes.

Product matching restrictions refers to the challenge of delivering the exact same product back to the customer after it has been repaired or updated. For some products this is not relevant, whereas for others it is crucial; e.g. computers and mobile phones with personal data.

The uncertainty of necessary.... is a challenge to operations and cycle management. The "routings" in operations are set up after a worst-case-scenario, but it is only rarely a product needs to undergo all steps in the process. Hence larger than necessary cycle times for products and unnecessary transportation of products is the result.

As per the above, it is obvious that Reverse Logistics introduces many new challenges to global logistics managers, that are different from the challenges of forward logistics.

When designing the Reverse Logistics network manager, must pay attention to a number of factors. The most important are, legislation, customer value, incentives, speed and costs. First of all, if the industry is regulated by legislation, the Reverse Logistics network obviously has to comply with the legislation. Secondly it is quintessential for the logistics managers to consider how the Reverse Logistics system can optimize the value delivered to customers, for example where to locate "return-centers", what requirements to have for product returns (lenient return policy will increase perceived customer service, but may increase costs) and how to deliver information to customers. Designing the right incentives for customers to return products are extremely important. Having the right incentives will lead to a larger and, ceteris paribus, more stable and predictable supply of products – remember that the unstable and unpredictable supply of products caused most of the challenges to begin with. If the cycle time in the Reverse Logistics network is to slow it will not only decrease customer value, but also increase the risk of obsolescence products. Also, speed is important when considering that what the company can resell – does not need to be produced. Lastly, the logistics manager has to consider costs. As always, the manager has to do a cost/benefit analysis. I.e. does the reverse Logistics Network add benefit or would it be cheaper to produce the product from scrap. Also, important to design KPI's and cost drivers, to monitor and see where costs actually incur. (Tatham, 2011)

6.0 Conclusion

From the above it can be concluded that Reverse Logistics is a challenge for global logistics managers in the current, medium and most likely long term.

Legislation and CSR expectations and requirements from stakeholders were identified as the main external drivers. Competition, clearing channels, value recapturing and asset recovery were identified as the main internal motives for firms to pursue establishment of a Reverse Logistics network.

The benefits of establishing a successful Reverse Logistics network were found to be many. Especially the added customer value, securing scarce resources, lower costs and reduced cycle times were found attractive.

Furthermore the differences between forward logistics and Reverse Logistics were highlighted to build an understanding of the challenges global logistics managers face, in order to achieve the benefits.

As with the benefits, the challenges are many. Especially the fact that the Reverse Logistic network is supply driven, leads to managerial challenges, due to the unstable and unpredictable supply conditions. Customer incentives which can mitigate the challenge of unstable demand, was found to be among the five most important features of a Reverse Logistics network. The other four were, network design, customer value, speed and cost management.

As a final conclusion, what should be taken from this research report is that Reversed Logistics are here to stay. With proper and due diligence management Reverse Logistics can be turned into a profit centre instead of, as it often is now, a cost centre.

References

Burke, L. & Logsdon, J.M. (1996). How Corporate Social responsibility Pays Off. *Long range Planning.* 4(29), 495-502.

Cuevas, S 2011, *Climate change, vulnerability, and risk linkages*, International Journal of Climate Change Strategies and Management, vol. 3 no. 1, pp.29 – 60 Emerald Group Publishing Limited

Deffree S., (2008) *Ontario begins WEEE directive complianc.* Supply Chain, Reed Business Information, a division of Reed Elsevier, Inc, Vol 53, Issue 5, p. 72.

Dutton G., 2010. *Reverse Logistics: money tree or money pit? Streamlining the returns process makes money and cuts costs.* World Trade Journal, Vol. 23, Issue 7, p.28

Guide, Jr., Jayaraman, V., Srivastava, R., Benton, W. C. (2000). *Supply-Chain Management for Recoverable Manufacturing Systems*, Interfaces, Vol. 30, Issue 3, pp. 125-142.

Gupta, S & Sharma, N. (2009). CSR- A Business Opportunity. *The Indian Journal of Industrial Relations,* 3(44).

Halldorson A., 2008. *Reverse Logistics.* Supply Management, Vol 13, Issue 3, p. 26.

Hawks, K. (2006), *What is Reverse Logistics?*, Reverse Logistics Magazine, Winter/Spring p. 12, 15 & 21.

Kokkinaki, A.I., Dekker, R., de Koster, M.B.M., Pappis, C., Verbeke, W. (2002) *E-Business Models for Reverse Logistics: Contributions and Challenges*, Proceedings of the International Conference on Information Technology: Coding and Computing, pp. 470-476.

Kwan Tan, A. W., Kumar, A. (2006) *A decision making model for reverse ligistics in the computer industry.* The international journal of Logistics Management, Vol 17, No 3, p 331-354.

Mollenkopf, D, Stolze, H, Tate, W & Ueltschy, M 2010, *Green, lean and global supply chain,* International Journal of Physical Distribution & Logistics Management, vol. 40 no. 1/2 pp. 14-41, Emerald Group Publishing Limited

Lourenço, H., Soto, J. P. (2002), *A Recoverable Production Planning Model*, UPF Economics and Business Working Paper No. 636, 41 pages.

Peters, R. & Mullen, M.R. (2009). Some Evidence of the Cumulative Effects of Corporate Social Responsibility on Financial Performance. *The Journal of Global Business Issues*, (3),1-14.

Rivlin, K., Brisson, J.P., & Wharwood (2005), D. *Preparing for the WEEE Directive.* Printed Circuit Design and Manufacture, Volume 22, Issue 4, p. 34

Rogers, D. S., Tibben-Lembke, R. S. (1998), *Going Backwards: Reverse Logistics Trends and Practices,* RLEC Press, Pittsburgh, PA., 283 pages.

Rogers, D. S., Tibben-Lembke, R. S. (2002), *Differences between forward and reverse logistics in a retail environment,* Supply Chain Management: An International Journal, Vol. 7, No. 5, pp. 271 – 282.

Shen, C. & Chang, Y. (2009). Ambition Versus Conscience, Does Corporate Social Responsibility Pay off? The Application of Matching methods. *Journal of Business Ethics,* (88), 133-153.

Skinner, L. R., Bryant, P. T., Richey, R. G. (2008), *Examining the impact of reverse logistics disposition strategies,* International Journal of Physical Distribution & Logistics Management, Vol. 38, No. 7, pp. 518-540.

Smith, A. D. (2005) *Reverse logistics programs: gauging their effects on CRM and online behavior,* The journal of information and knowledge management systems, Vol. 35 No. 3, pp. 166-181.

Soto Zulaga, J.P.S (2005), *Reverse Logistics: Models and Application.* Department of Economics and Business, Universititat Pompeu Fabra, 192 pages.

Tatham, P. H. (2011), *Strategic Supply Chain Course Material*

Tibben-Lembke, R. S. (2002), *Life after death: reverse logistics and the product life cycle,* International Journal of Physical Distribution & Logistics Management, Vol. 32, No. 3, pp. 223-245.

Tierney S., 2004. *Wincanton reverses into the future.* Supply Chain Europe, vol 13, issue 8, p.32.

Weele, A. V. (2010). *Purchasing and Supply Chain Management,* Thomas Rennie- Cengage Learning.

WEEE Directive: European Parliament 2003, Viewed 28 October 2011. *http://eur-lex.europa.eu/LexUriServ/LexUriServ.do?uri=CELEX:32002L0096:en:HTML*